Our Shared World

Aviva Werner

BEHRMAN HOUSE

Behrman House, Inc.
www.behrmanhouse.com

Dedicated to my father, Jeffrey Zablow.

Aviva Werner

Design: **Jill A. Winitzer, WinitzerDesign.com**

The publisher gratefully acknowledges the following sources of photographs and graphic images:
(T=top, B=bottom, L=left, R=rigth)
Cover JBryson/iStockPhoto; ii Camilo Torres/Shutterstock; 2 Konstantin Chagin/Shutterstock; 3 Ashley van Dyck/Shutterstock; 6 Christos Georghiou/Shutterstock; 7, 37 Israel GPO; 11, 21, 31, 41 Lena Sergeeva/Shutterstock; 12 marekuliasz/Shutterstock; 13 owen1978/Shutterstock; 14TL Feng Yu/Shutterstock; 14BL Steve Lovegrove/Shutterstock; 14TR Anneka/Shutterstock; 14BR Monkey Business Images/Shutterstock; 16, 36 Antonio Abrignani/Shutterstock; 17 American Jewish Historical Society; 20 agsandrew/Shutterstock; 22 Hein Nouwens/Shutterstock; 23 Fabio Berti/Shutterstock; 26 ruskpp/Shutterstock; 27 Michael Freund; 32 Sergey Nivens/Shutterstock; 33 amasterphotographer/Shutterstock; 34 Robert Adrian Hillman/Shutterstock; 40 Pavel Vakhrushev/Shutterstock

Copyright ©2013 Behrman House, Inc.
Springfield, New Jersey
ISBN 978-0-87441-873-6
Manufactured in the United States of America

  Library of Congress Cataloging-in-Publication Data
Werner, Aviva.
  Our shared world / Aviva Werner.
      page. cm -- (Living Jewish values ; volume 4)
  ISBN 978-0-87441-873-6
  1. Jewish religious education--Textbooks for children. 2. Communities--Religious aspects--Judaism--Textbooks. 3. Justice--Religious aspects--Judaism--Textbooks. 4. Responsibility--Religious aspects--Judaism--Textbooks. 5. Jewish ethics--Textbooks. 6. Jewish way of life--Textbooks. I. Title.
  BM105.W47 2013
  296.7083--dc23
                              2012043326

CONTENTS

INTRODUCTION

Every seven years during the Temple period, the entire nation gathered in Jerusalem for the mitzvah of *hak'heil*. The *kohanim* (priests) would fan out through the city, blowing golden trumpets to assemble the crowds and bring them to the Holy Temple. The king, in all his royal finery, would sit atop a wooden platform in the Temple courtyard and read selections from the Torah to the assembled masses. Given that attendance at this ceremony was mandatory for all Jews—men, women, and children—*hak'heil* was an awesome display of Jewish unity and a powerful statement of communal purpose.

The traditional *hak'heil* was discontinued after the destruction of the Second Temple but was revived by the State of Israel as a symbolic assembly. In place of the king, the president of Israel reads the Torah portions. Large and small gatherings are also held in synagogues and homes throughout the world as a display of Jewish unity and commitment to Torah.

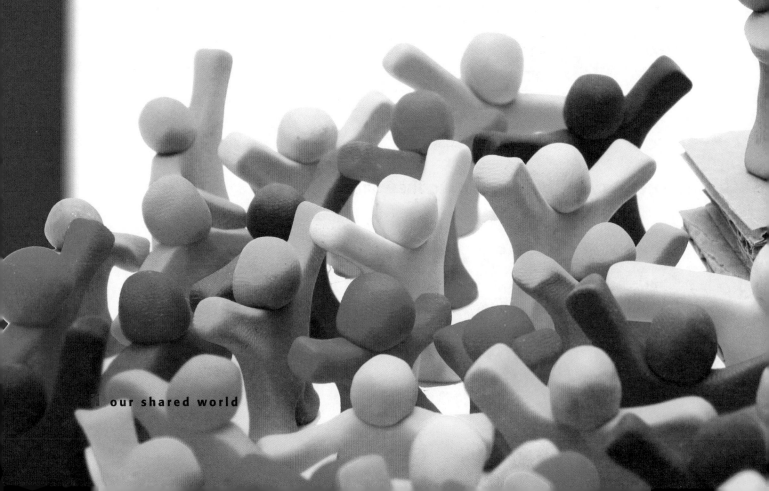

This book, *Our Shared World*, is volume 4 in the *Living Jewish Values* series. In it, we will study four values that help us connect with our community:

Kehillah—Community
Tzedek—Justice
Arevut—Mutual Responsibility
Tikkun Olam—Repairing the World

Each chapter features legends, personality quizzes, role-model profiles, activities, and journal prompts to make the learning interesting and enjoyable. As you read this book, you'll consider your commitment to the Jewish community, the benefits you can reap from belonging, and ways that you can contribute your talents and time for the greater good. Consider this book your personal trumpet call to gather together with your local community and the global Jewish community in a display of commitment to others and to God.

CHAPTER 1

Kehillah

Nearly three months after their first tastes of freedom, throngs of former Israelite slaves arrived at the wilderness of Sinai. These were people who had witnessed the Ten Plagues and the splitting of the sea. They were nourished by the manna, and their thirst was quenched by water from a rock. Their travels were guided by the Clouds of Glory, and conversations with God had become their new norm. Now, at the foot of Mount Sinai, they erected their tents and unpacked their belongings, eager to receive God's Torah and become God's nation. *(Exodus)*

Community

At Mount Sinai, three million former slaves were transformed into a community, or קְהִילָה (*kehillah*). Among their ranks were distinct tribes and families, and people of all different ages and abilities, united in their commitment to each other and to God. Since then, Jewish communities continue to work to provide for the spiritual and social needs of their members. Each of us has a unique role to play within the community, but together we benefit from belonging to a thriving and vibrant Jewish society.

JEWISH DIVERSITY

Community thrives on diversity. There was much diversity among the twelve tribes that stood at the foot of Mount Sinai. The Jewish community today also celebrates diversity— geographic, racial, philosophical, economic, and cultural. There are Jews of all colors, shapes, and sizes, Jews by birth and Jews by choice, Jews with disabilities and Jews with an array of talents and interests. Despite our differences that have the potential to divide, we have an obligation to respect one another and to treat each other with dignity. By celebrating our commonalities and recognizing ourselves in other Jews, we strengthen the Jewish community.

ACTIVITY 1

We all belong to a variety of communities. Some are microcosms of the larger Jewish community; others are distinct and separate from each other. Below is a list of communities to which you may belong. Add any that are not listed. Draw a diagram to illustrate how your circles of belonging are related to each other.

For example, your school and classroom may be related like this, since one is a microcosm of the other:

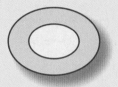

Your sports team and orchestra may be related like this, since they are not connected:

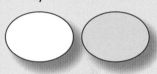

However, if the sports team and orchestra are both part of your school community, this part of your diagram may look like this:

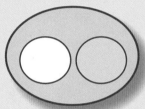

Jewish school

Secular school

Classroom

Grade

Synagogue

Youth group

Camp

Bunk

Sports team

Choir

Orchestra or band

Hobby club

Social network

Community service group

Scouting troop

What Makes You Feel Like Part of the Team?

Take this quiz and find out.

Your favorite part of playing on the soccer team is:

◆ The lasting friendships that you've made during the season.

◆ The music you play on your iPod during warm-ups before games.

◆ The bus rides home, when you all let loose and make each other laugh.

When you think about Shabbat at summer camp, you long for:

◆ The Shabbat atmosphere that you and your friends create.

◆ The nice clothes you wear as a sign of respect for the beauty of the day.

◆ The beautiful service, with everyone praying together to welcome the Sabbath Queen.

At this year's Celebrate Israel Parade, you can't wait for:

◆ The high you'll get, surrounded by so many people showing their love for Israel.

◆ The sea of people from all over, waving the same blue-and-white flag.

◆ The Hebrew songs the crowd will all sing together.

Your class raised $5,000 for tzedakah, and you're overjoyed thinking about:

◆ What a difference that money is going to make for the needy.

◆ The TV your class bought for the kids in the homeless shelter.

◆ How hard you all worked together to raise that money.

Mostly red
Championship game

Working toward a final goal or sharing a common purpose unites you with others. Sometimes it means putting aside personal differences, and other times it means learning to see things the same way, but it always means a solid team effort. You love the feeling of success, the thrill of victory, and the bond you feel with those who helped you get there.

Mostly green
Team uniform

Sharing tangible, practical things—like a school ring—ties you to others. Even when you don't see obvious similarities between yourself and others, you find some ways to connect with them. As Solomon says in Proverbs 22:2, "The rich and poor meet together; God is the Maker of them all."

Mostly blue
Practice session

Whether it's a weekly ritual or a chance encounter, shared experiences bond you to others in your community. You know that the journey is the best part of the trip, including all the ups and downs along the way. The words of King David speak to you: "How good and pleasant it is for siblings to sit together in unity" *(Psalm 133:1).*

AGADDIC TRADITION

Every person can connect to God individually through prayer. However, Judaism teaches that when a community comes together for communal prayer in a minyan (a group of ten Jewish adults), the prayer is much more powerful. The following parable illustrates why this is so.

A new king was crowned in a certain country. As part of his coronation, he would travel to two towns in the kingdom. The town council of each municipality met to decide how they would greet their new ruler in order to find favor in his eyes.

Town A decided to send a special gift to the king each day leading up to the visit. In this way, the gifts from Town A would be spread out over the course of a week. Town B decided to gather many gifts for the king and present them all on the day of his visit. In this way, they hoped to impress the king with a sizeable collection of riches.

As the king's carriage traveled toward Town A, a messenger arrived each day bearing the town's daily gift. And each day the king found fault with the gift from the first town. None of the gifts were perfect, and he couldn't help but focus on what they lacked. However, when the king arrived at Town B and was presented with a mountain of gifts, he was overwhelmed by the generosity of the town council. Yes, none of the gifts were perfect, but he didn't examine each one individually. Instead, he enjoyed seeing the tower of gifts that were collected in his honor.

When we pray on our own, God is surely pleased. But we are imperfect, each with our faults. On the other hand, when we unite in a minyan, God sees us as a group, a united community, and overlooks our individual shortcomings.

ACTIVITY 2

The literal meaning of the term *beit knesset*, synagogue, is "a place where people meet." What does this tell you about prayer? _____
_____

In your experience, what are the benefits of communal prayer? _____
_____

Write your own original parable to explain one of the benefits of communal prayer. _____
_____
_____
_____
_____

KEHILLAH SUPERSTAR: ELIEZER BEN YEHUDA

His neighbors thought he was crazy. "You fool!" they shouted. "Hebrew is for prayer only. Do you really think our ancient tongue will ever be spoken on the streets?" Eliezer Ben Yehuda didn't flinch. "*Kein* [yes]," he replied.

From the day he settled in Jerusalem in 1881, Ben Yehuda believed that reviving spoken Hebrew would unify the diverse Jewish community in the Holy Land. Unmoved by his neighbors' doubts, he launched his ambitious plan at home, forcing his wife, Devorah, to speak only Hebrew in the house.

She tried her best, but when their son Ben Zion was four years old and had not spoken a single word, Devorah worried that he might never speak; after all, his father constantly invented new words and spent all day recording them in his dictionary. Moreover, when guests visited, Ben Yehuda sent the boy to his bedroom, "to keep his ears free of 'foreign' tongues," his father insisted.

One day, Ben Yehuda berated his wife for singing a Russian lullaby to their son. "How dare you betray me like this!" he shouted. "Don't you realize how important Hebrew is?" He slumped into a chair, and then, unable to contain himself, he leapt up, a clenched fist raised in the air. Devorah burst into tears. Overwhelmed by his parents' argument, Ben Zion opened his mouth to protest, and his words emerged in Hebrew.

Soon, Hebrew poured out of Ben Yehuda's home into the streets, the schools, and the entire nation. Spoken Hebrew, whose revival was untiringly pioneered by Eliezer Ben Yehuda, continues to unite not only the diverse Jewish community in Israel, but the entire Jewish community around the globe.

> "If a language which has stopped being spoken, with nothing remaining of it save what remains of our language—if there is such a language—can return and be the spoken tongue of an individual for all necessities of his life, there is no room for doubt that it can become the spoken language of a community."

Learn the Lingo

Definition: *group of ten or more Jewish adults gathered for prayer*

Explanation in your own words:

Minyan

Use it in a sentence:

How it applies to your life:

Definition: *literally "collective," a unique type of community found only in Israel. In a traditional kibbutz, community members share everything and work together toward a common goal.*

List one benefit of collective living:

Kibbutz

Use it in a sentence:

List one drawback to collective living:

Complete the following charts with information about each *kehillah* vocabulary word. The definition has been completed for you.

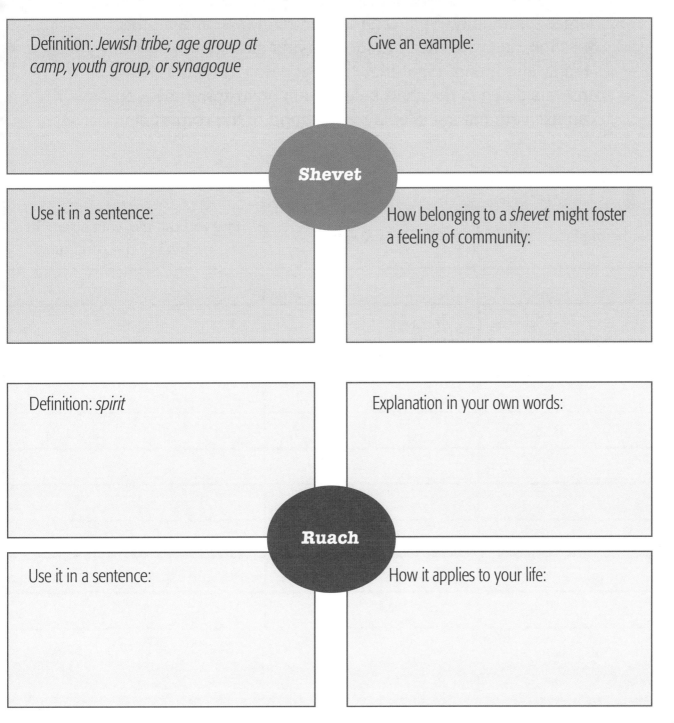

Definition: *Jewish tribe; age group at camp, youth group, or synagogue*

Give an example:

Shevet

Use it in a sentence:

How belonging to a *shevet* might foster a feeling of community:

Definition: *spirit*

Explanation in your own words:

Ruach

Use it in a sentence:

How it applies to your life:

ACTIVITY 3

Every person brings something unique and personal to the larger community. What can you contribute? To answer this question, first you'll need to identify your strengths. Ask your family and friends what they think you do well. Write their answers down in the chart below, then brainstorm how you can use your natural talents for the good of the community.

Name of person asked	Your strengths	How you can use your strengths to contribute to the community

WHAT I THINK

"A bundle of reeds cannot be broken by a person; but, taken one by one, even a child can break them." *(Midrash Tanchuma Nitzavim)*

1. In what ways are you like a reed in the text? How are you bound together with others? In what ways are you independent and separate from others?

2. What happens when your beliefs or opinions conflict with communal norms? How can we make different opinions heard and still maintain respect?

3. Keep an eye out for community events in your synagogue, school, or neighborhood. Try to attend at least two community events that interest you.

4. Draw a map of your community. Label the places that are most important to you.

5. Is an online social network a community? Explain your answer.

CHAPTER 2

Tzedek

The angels disguised as men left Abraham's tent, headed in the direction of Sodom. They would destroy the city, which was steeped in sin, and all its residents. When Abraham found out about the impending annihilation, he couldn't believe it. "What if there should be righteous people in the midst of the city?" he argued with God. "It would be sacrilege to bring death upon the righteous along with the wicked. Shall the Judge of all the earth not deal justly?" And God replied, "If I find in Sodom fifty righteous people, then I would spare the entire place on their account."

(Genesis 18:16–26)

Justice

In this case, Abraham and God argued a case of life and death. They were in the desert, not a courtroom, but they decided the fate of a city and its people, something modern lawmakers do all the time. Which was right, exacting judgment on the wicked or having compassion for the innocent? The Torah commands us to pursue צֶדֶק (*tzedek*), a vision of a fair and just world. Judaism realizes that *tzedek* requires a combination of strict letter-of-the-law judgment and merciful compassion. Many Jewish laws give us direction toward *tzedek*. These include the laws of *tzedakah*, which require us to help others fulfill their basic human needs, and other laws of ethical behavior.

The Jewish concept of justice is not limited to legal arguments. Rather, it is a vision of a fair and just world. This vision extends to our families, our schools, and our communities. We must seek out opportunities to correct injustices big and small and to do our part to increase *tzedek*.

RULES AND REGULATIONS

Justice isn't just for the courtroom, and laws aren't only found in legal books. Rules are essential elements in our daily lives. They define everything from how we play basketball to how we are expected to behave in the classroom and at the dinner table. Although we are created in the image of God, we are not perfect. We need systems that keep us fair and honest and allow us to correct and learn from our mistakes. A true sense of *tzedek* requires us to clearly understand not only the rules themselves, but why following them is meaningful in our lives and a benefit to society.

ACTIVITY 1

Here are some of the 613 rules, or *mitzvot*, in the Torah. For each one listed below, explain how to follow the Jewish rule and why we need it.

Give tzedakah.

_____

_____

_____

_____

Put a mezuzah on each doorpost.

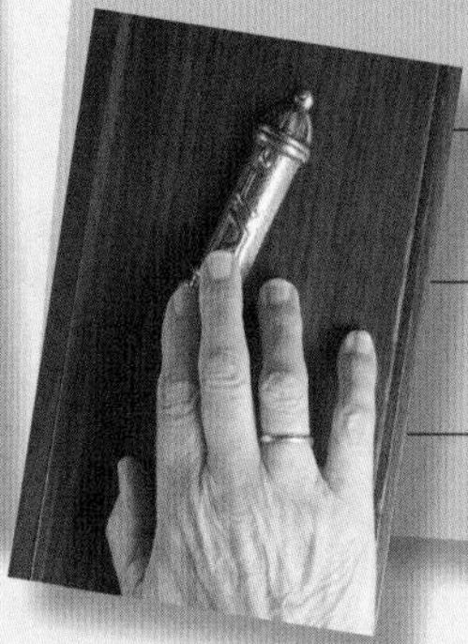

_____

_____

_____

_____

Do not steal.

_____

_____

_____

_____

Respect your father and mother.

_____

_____

_____

_____

So You Think You Can Make a Difference?

Take this quiz and find out.

You resent the way a new TV show portrays a Jewish character. You:

◆ Attend a Diversity Day rally in town.

◆ Create a website that highlights video clips of the worst examples of negative stereotyping, and then e-mail links to everyone you know.

◆ Refuse to watch the show, and when your friends talk about it, tell them what you think.

The school concert is approaching, and you know that some kids can't afford to go. You:

◆ Distribute flyers to spread the word about a fundraiser your friends have organized.

◆ Organize a car wash fundraiser to lower the cost for everyone.

◆ Contribute your allowance to the concert fund collection.

You read an article condemning child slavery on chocolate plantations in Africa. You:

◆ Attend a local rally organized to publicize such atrocities.

◆ Call your local grocery store and urge the manager to stop buying products made from chocolate harvested by child slaves.

◆ Donate one week's allowance to an advocacy group that is lobbying Congress to act.

The boys' teams are assigned to play on better fields than the girls' teams—again. You:

◆ Agree to go with a small group to meet with the coach.

◆ Organize a meeting of all the teams and coaches to discuss the matter.

◆ Send a letter to the coach, describing why you think the setup is unfair.

Mostly red
Actor
You are happy to participate, lending yourself and your voice to help a just communal cause. In Deuteronomy *(16:20)*, we are taught to follow (or pursue) justice: "Justice, justice, you shall pursue."

Mostly green
Director
Like a director, you take charge and show others in your community how to act. You know what's right, taking to heart the words of Isaiah: "Learn to do good. Devote yourself to justice; aid the wronged" *(Isaiah 1:17)*.

Mostly blue
Behind-the-scenes worker
You personally embrace the vigorous pursuit of justice and believe that your actions, however small, will make a difference in the community. As Hillel said, "If I am not for myself, who is for me? If I am only for myself, what am I? And if not now, when?" *(Pirkei Avot 1:14)*.

AGADDIC TRADITION

"**We should demand** a portion in the land. It's our late father's right."

"Noa," responded Hoglah, "we can't just barge into the Tent of Meeting and make demands of Moses. We need a plan."

"Hoglah's right," answered Milcah. "We must speak to Moses, Elazar the Priest, and the leaders of the entire assembly, but timing is crucial to our case. Let's wait until tomorrow when they will be expounding on the laws of levirate marriage."

"Brilliant idea!" exclaimed Tirzah. "We can show the leaders how the laws of levirate marriage and of inheritance contradict each other when it comes to the status of daughters."

"In the meantime, let's study the laws ourselves," suggested Mahlah. "Our reasoning must be razor-sharp and must take into account all the relevant laws if we are to succeed."

"For the sake of our father's memory, may God, whose compassion extends to men and women alike, bless our efforts," prayed Milcah.

The five sisters set out for the Tent of Meeting the next day, sharing memories of their father and reviewing their legal arguments as they walked. Before long they stood before the leaders of Israel.

"We are the daughters of Zelophehad, son of Hepher," they began. "Our father died in the wilderness, but he was not among the assembly of Korach that gathered against God. We come before you today because our father had no sons. Why should our father's name be omitted from among his family because he had no son? We ask that you give us an inheritance in the Promised Land among our father's brothers."

Empathizing with the sisters, Moses brought their claim before God, whose verdict wasn't long in coming: "The daughters of Zelophehad speak properly. You shall cause the inheritance of their father to pass over to them. If a man dies and he has no son, his inheritance shall pass to his daughter. This shall be for the children of Israel as a decree of justice."

ACTIVITY 2

What compelled Zelophehad's daughters to petition for a change in the law?

_____

_____

What strategies did they use when preparing their arguments? _____

_____

_____

How might we follow their example when petitioning for change? _____

_____

_____

TZEDEK SUPERSTAR: JUSTINE WISE POLIER

As the sun set over Passaic, New Jersey, thousands of women streamed into the streets. Dressed in stained, sweaty rags, they trudged toward the textile mills for the night shift. Justine Wise Polier, daughter of powerful labor activist Rabbi Stephen Wise, walked with them, disguised as a new immigrant. *My feet are killing me from last night's shift,* she thought, *but it's worth it to experience what these women suffer.*

Like lifeless puppets, the women dragged themselves up narrow, stuffy stairs. They stood around their worktables, where the mill owners forced them to work for ten hours straight.

"Roll call!" barked the mill boss. "Waterman?"

"Here," Justine said, responding to her mother's maiden name. *I hope he doesn't figure out my real name. I shudder to think what might happen if the bosses knew my father was their biggest enemy.*

Roll call continued, but Justine could no longer hear the names. The skinny blonde girl, who always wore the dirty red scarf around her neck, started coughing uncontrollably. *That's a sure sign of tuberculosis,* Justine thought. *She's spreading the bacteria everywhere.*

Despite the dangerous conditions, Justine worked undercover for months, until the evening when the bosses discovered her true identify. Standing up to three intimidating goons who demanded she get out immediately, Justine snapped, "You'll see me again—and when you do, I'll bring you to justice for forcing such terrible conditions on your workers."

True to her word, Justine returned two years later to support Passaic's great textile strike. Hoisted on a platform above the crowd, she raised her voice against injustice, inspiring the mill workers to go on strike. In December 1927, the textile workers finally won the right to unionize. Justine went on to become the first woman judge in New York State in 1935.

> "I don't believe we can have justice without caring, or caring without justice. These are inseparable aspects of life and work for children as they are for adults."

Learn the Lingo

Definition: *Jewish law*

How it contrasts with secular law:

Halachah

Use it in a sentence:

How it applies to your life:

Definition: *trying to peacefully resolve a dispute through the help of an outside party*

A time you were involved in mediation:

Mediation

Use it in a sentence:

How it can build community:

Complete the following charts with information about each *tzedek* vocabulary word. The definition has been completed for you.

Definition: *righteous giving of charity*

Charitable causes that speak to you:

Tzedakah

Use it in a sentence:

How it applies to your life:

Definition: *righteous person*

Example of a *tzaddik* you know:

Tzaddik

Use it in a sentence:

How it applies to your life:

ACTIVITY 3

Develop your own action plan and speak up against an injustice in your community.

Personal Action Plan Outline

Description of an injustice	
What is already being done to address this issue?	
What can I do to make a difference? (Options, contact information, and other relevant details)	
Step-by-step action plan	1. 2. 3.

Examples of injustices you may consider addressing: discrimination, prejudice, oppression, sexism, racism, wealth discrimination, homelessness.

WHAT I THINK

"If one can protest the misdeeds of one's household, yet does not, the person becomes guilty with them. If a person can protest the misdeeds of one's townspeople and does not, the person is guilty with them. If one can protest the misdeeds of the entire world and does not, that person is guilty with them." *(Talmud, Shabbat 54b)*

1. How can protesting help right injustices? Why should you protest even if people won't listen?

2. . What is the role of courage in the pursuit of justice? How can we grapple with fear that affects our willingness to pursue a cause?

3. Learn more about a Jewish figure who fought for justice. Choose a social activist, lawyer, judge, rabbi, fundraiser, or organizer. What was his or her view of justice? What values motivated him or her to pursue justice?

4. Clip articles from the newspaper about *tzedek* and share them with the class.

CHAPTER 3

Arevut

Four passengers clambered onto a rowboat, careful not to tip it over. One passenger untied the rope that tethered the boat to the dock, then another rowed the boat toward the center of the river. Meanwhile, a third passenger took a drill out of his backpack and began to make a hole beneath his seat. "What in the world are you doing?" cried the others. The man with the drill was undeterred. "What's it your business? I'm only drilling under myself." His fellow passengers answered in a panic, "But you will flood the boat for all of us!" *(Leviticus Rabbah 4:6)*

Mutual Responsibility

Our actions—even those that are small and seemingly private—can have a huge impact on the entire community. עֲרֵבוּת (*arevut*) means that we as Jews are interdependent. Because of our collective history, Jews share a mutual responsibility and destiny. We have a duty to help other Jews when we can, learning to pay attention to others, to anticipate and respond to their needs, and to be dependable. *Arevut* implies a special obligation to the State of Israel, oppressed Jews, and Jewish communities at risk, too. Like the passengers in the rowboat, we must interest ourselves not only in our own behavior, but in the behavior of our friends, our schools, and our communities, because we are all in the same boat. We are inherently one.

HATRED AND LOVE

Arevut is like glue that binds one Jew to another. Baseless hatred, when one Jew hates another for no good reason, has the power to destroy that bond of mutual responsibility. Baseless hatred means being mean to a classmate because she has an annoying habit, she doesn't dress right, or she's more or less religious than you are. It's treating another Jew as the enemy, when really she is family. We can combat baseless hatred, and thereby increase our feelings of *arevut*, by practicing baseless love.

ACTIVITY 1

Jews around the world are united by our shared values, culture, and history. On the lines of the fishbone diagram, write three things you have in common with Jews everywhere in each category.

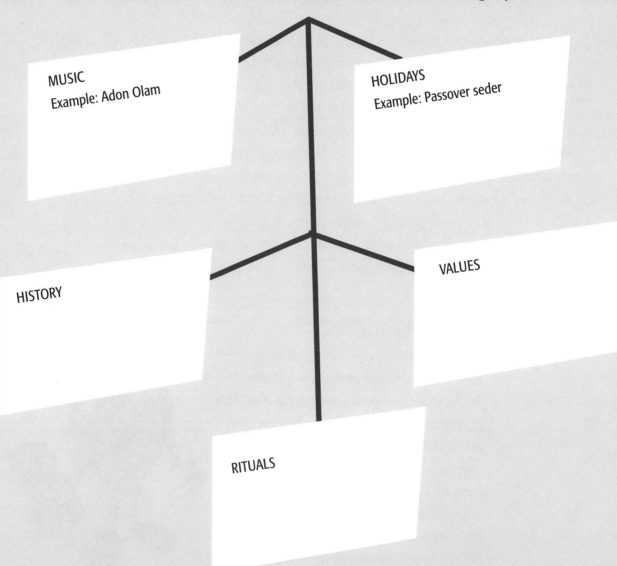

MUSIC
Example: Adon Olam

HOLIDAYS
Example: Passover seder

HISTORY

VALUES

RITUALS

What else do you have in common with Jews all over the world? _____
_____
_____

How Do You Set the Stage?

Take this quiz and find out.

Your basketball team has lost three games in a row. What do you do?

◆ You stand up for your teammates when the class bully tries to make them feel bad.

◆ You work to improve your game by practicing your jump shot.

◆ You make up a funny cheer to raise the team's spirit.

Your family is hosting a block party. You:

◆ Help the elderly woman down the street join by pushing her wheelchair.

◆ Take charge of the entertainment for the little kids.

◆ Make invitations encouraging everyone to attend.

Your class is leading services during Youth Shabbat at your synagogue. You:

◆ Go over the services with kids who have difficulty reading Hebrew.

◆ Volunteer to write a play about the *parashah* to perform for the younger children.

◆ Leave a note in everyone's siddur wishing them good luck on the big day.

Your youth group president is so busy with schoolwork that she hasn't started organizing the upcoming event. You:

◆ Listen when she tells you how stressed out she feels.

◆ Offer to begin planning the event yourself, since your homework is already finished.

◆ Remind her about the event and tell her you're sure it'll be great.

Mostly red
Support staff
You stand by others in easy and difficult times. As the Torah says, "You shall not harden your heart nor shut your hand from your poor friend" *(Deuteronomy 15:7).*

Mostly green
Backup
You know how to take your turn doing hard tasks and how to share leadership. As King Solomon said, "For everything there is a season and a time for every purpose under the heavens" *(Ecclesiastes 3:1).*

Mostly blue
Cheering squad
You are encouraging and supportive. "Two are better than one … for if they fall, the one can lift up the other" *(Ecclesiastes 4:9–10).*

AGADDIC TRADITION

It was an act of war. The nation of Amalek, descended from Esau, heard of the miraculous deliverance of the Jewish nation from Egypt and immediately set out to destroy it. The Amalekite army snuck up from behind and slaughtered the weakest Israelites bringing up the rear of the traveling band.

In response, Moses instructed Joshua to assemble an army to fight Amalek. While the new recruits would fight with swords and spears, Moses and the rest of the nation would wage a spiritual battle. Moses, Aaron, and Hur ascended to the top of the hill, where Moses raised his hands to the sky, signaling Israel to look heavenward and pray to God. As long as Moses's hands were raised high, Israel was stronger in battle, but when Moses lowered his arms, Amalek became stronger.

When Moses's hands became tired, they put a stone under him as a seat. Moses sat, and Aaron and Hur held up his arms, one on the right side and one on the left, enabling Moses to keep his hands up in faithful prayer until sunset.

Our sages wonder why Moses had to sit on a stone for all those hours. Didn't they have a chair or a cushion for him to sit more comfortably? They answer that Moses was motivated by a feeling of *arevut*. Israel was fighting a bloody battle, and Moses chose to share in the distress of his nation.

ACTIVITY 2

Do you think people should put themselves into distress to understand the problems faced by another? _____
_____
_____

What does personal experience add to our understanding of another's pain? _____
_____
_____

How might we follow Moses's example to share in the distress of our fellow Jews? _____
_____
_____

AREVUT SUPERSTAR: MICHAEL FREUND

In the village of Churachandpur in a remote region of India's northeast, a group of men gather in the synagogue for daily morning prayers. They rise at prescribed times and face toward Jerusalem in the west. According to their tradition, these members of the Bnei Menashe are descended from one of the Ten Lost Tribes of Israel. Their ancestors were separated from the rest of the Jewish world over twenty-seven hundred years ago, yet the Bnei Menashe steadfastly maintained their Jewish traditions and culture. They circumcised baby boys on the eighth day, observed Shabbat, and were careful about kashrut. They also established cities of refuge as described in the Torah and painted their doorposts with blood for their holiday of deliverance, which was celebrated around the time of Passover.

Today, thanks to the efforts of Michael Freund and his organization Shavei Israel, thousands of Bnei Menashe are returning to the Jewish people and even settling in Israel. In 2005, at Michael's request, Israel's Sephardic Chief Rabbi formally recognized members of the Bnei Menashe community as descendants of the Jewish people and helped bring many of them to the Holy Land. Michael's organization guides the Bnei Menashe through the *aliyah* process, helps them learn Hebrew, and teaches them all about Judaism. There are now Bnei Menashe immigrants serving in the Israel Defense Forces, working as scribes and rabbis, and growing in their Jewish knowledge and affiliation. "The Bnei Menashe are a blessing to the Jewish people and to the State of Israel," remarks Freund, "and they strengthen us no less than we do them."

In addition to his work with the Bnei Menashe, Michael has worked with lost and hidden Jewish communities in Spain, China, Poland, South America, and other unexpected places. Through Michael's efforts, these groups who were cut off from the Jewish people over the centuries are reconnecting with their Jewish roots and rejoining our Jewish community.

> "The saga of the Bnei Menashe is testimony to the power of Jewish history and Jewish memory. The Bnei Menashe clung to their identity despite twenty-seven centuries of wandering, never forgetting who they are or where they came from, even as they nourished the dream that one day they would return. Their story is our story, and it underscores our people's faith and resilience even in the most trying of circumstances."

Learn the Lingo

Definition: *the status of belonging to a particular nation*

How the term relates to community:

Nationality

Use it in a sentence:

Your nationality:

Definition: *the state of having little or no money*

Someone you know who fights poverty:

Poverty

Use it in a sentence:

How it applies to your life:

Complete the following charts with information about each *arevut* vocabulary word. The definition has been completed for you.

Definition: *a person who settles in a new country*	Someone you know who is an immigrant:
Use it in a sentence:	How an immigrant joins a new community:

Immigrant

Definition: *obligation to redeem (or rescue) Jewish captives and prisoners*	Example of a captive in history:
Use it in a sentence:	How you can help redeem captives:

Pidyon sh'vuyim

ACTIVITY 3

· ·

As a member of the Jewish community, your responsibilities are increasing as you get older. How do you currently participate in the community? What are your goals for community involvement in the future? Develop goals that are **SMART**: **S**pecific, **M**easurable, **A**chievable, **R**elevant, and **T**ime-oriented.

SMART GOAL-SETTING EXAMPLE

	less-SMART	SMART-er
Specific	I want to get involved at synagogue.	I'm going to attend synagogue services.
Measurable	I'm going to attend synagogue services.	I'm going to attend services every Friday night.
Achievable	I'm going to attend services every day.	I'm going to attend services twice a month.
Relevant	I'm going to attend services.	I'm going to participate in services.
Time-oriented	I'm going to attend services three times.	I'm going to attend services three times by June 30.

Immediate **SMART** goal: This year I will participate in the community by

Check (√) that your goal is __ **S**pecific __ **M**easurable ___ **A**chievable ___ **R**elevant ___ **T**ime-oriented

Short-term **SMART** goal: When I become bar or bat mitzvah, I will participate in the community by

Check (√) that your goal is __ **S**pecific __ **M**easurable ___ **A**chievable ___ **R**elevant ___ **T**ime-oriented

Long-term **SMART** goal: When I am an adult, I will participate in the community by

Check (√) that your goal is __ **S**pecific __ **M**easurable ___ **A**chievable ___ **R**elevant ___ **T**ime-oriented

WHAT I THINK

"All Jews are responsible for one another."
(Talmud, Sh'vuot 39a)

1. How would you answer someone who criticizes the value of *arevut* as being too particularistic, saying, "You Jews are too tight-knit; you should be concerned with anyone who suffers and not just Jews"?

2. Have you ever felt like an outsider? What made you feel more included?

3. "Adopt" a Jewish community in another part of the world. Learn about its history, leaders, and customs. Brainstorm ways to connect to Jewish kids in that community. What do you have in common with them? What are your differences?

4. Imagine that you are one of the founders of a new Jewish community. Compose a mission statement that articulates the community's values and purpose.

5. Organize a drive to raise money for needy Jewish families to use in their preparation and celebration of an upcoming Jewish holiday.

CHAPTER 4

Tikkun Olam

Isaac Luria was a prodigy. At the age of fifteen he was proficient in all the Talmud, and by age thirty-five he was the recognized authority in the mystical secrets of Kabbalah. Rabbi Luria then moved to the mystical city of Tzefat in Israel, where the local kabbalists turned to him as their sage and teacher. Perhaps Rabbi Luria's most well-known teaching is that humanity's job is to repair the world, a concept called *tikkun olam*.

Repairing the World

We **often use** the term תִּיקּוּן עוֹלָם (*tikkun olam*), repairing the world, to refer to social action. The concept of *tikkun olam*, though, stems from Rabbi Luria's kabbalistic teaching that, at Creation, God's divine light was contracted into vessels, some of which shattered and showered the world with their debris. It is our job to repair the vessels by gathering the lost shards and sparks of divine light.

Tikkun olam, then, represents people's responsibility for bettering the world. This value involves both fixing the problems of our communities—including hunger, disease, pollution, poverty, and crime—and repairing spiritual breaks in individuals by bettering ourselves. By approaching *tikkun olam* from both the social and personal sides, we engage in "repairing the world under God's rule," as it says in the Aleinu prayer.

SETTING A GOOD EXAMPLE

If an older brother or sister makes a mistake, their parents might admonish them for not setting a better example for their younger siblings. The prophets tell us that we, as Jews, are meant to set a good example for the rest of the nations, to be a "light for the nations," as they put it. We are meant to model *tikkun olam* by improving the world in the way that God specifies. At camp, at school, and in any of the communities to which we belong, our actions should be the model of a proper society.

ACTIVITY 1

Imagine that this is a map of your neighborhood. What might be a social need of the people in each of the locations listed? How might you be able to help them? One example has been completed for you.

GROCERY STORE

HOSPITAL

SCHOOL

PLAYGROUND

LIBRARY

SYNAGOGUE

SENIOR CENTER

LIBRARY _____

SCHOOL _____

SYNAGOGUE _____

HOSPITAL Children who are patients need entertainment. I could help by collecting games for them.

GROCERY STORE _____

PLAYGROUND _____

SENIOR CENTER _____

How Do You Fix the World?

Take this quiz and find out.

It's summertime and you're looking to volunteer for a great project:

◆ Being a "camp buddy" for a special needs student from your synagogue.

◆ Working to reduce pollution and protect endangered species.

◆ Planning a concert to raise money to fight poverty in Israel.

The bumper sticker you'd most likely paste on your locker says:

◆ "Got Torah?"

◆ "One Planet. One Future."

◆ "Everybody is guilty of the good they *didn't* do."

Tuesday night, you're double-booked, but you'd just hate to miss:

◆ A chance to pray with your friends for a teacher who is gravely ill.

◆ An "End Animal Torture" fundraising party to stop unnecessary animal testing.

◆ A documentary about the genocide in Darfur, where thousands of innocent people are suffering.

When Earth Day rolls around, your class is organizing a special *tikkun olam* project. You chair the committee to:

◆ Write a *d'var Torah* to share with your classmates about the importance of *tikkun olam*.

◆ Coordinate a school-wide recycling program to save paper, plastic, and cans from trashing up our earth.

◆ Clean up the playground in a low-income neighborhood so kids can have a safe place to play.

Mostly red
Spiritual

The spiritual realm is where you are making a difference. You take to heart the words of Pirkei Avot 1:2, "The world stands on three things: on the Torah, on the service of God, and on acts of loving-kindness," and you are dedicated to repairing the world through all three.

Mostly green
Environment

The environment is where you put your efforts. As it says in Psalm 115:16, "God has given the earth to humanity," and you feel responsible to care for our land, water, and animals and to teach others to do the same.

Mostly blue
Social action

Social action is your focus. You're always asking, "If I am only for myself, what am I?" You can't ignore people's suffering and feel the push to repair the world by doing community service. In your fight for justice, you feel more connected to other people around the world.

AGADDIC TRADITION

Rabbi Beroka enjoyed spending the occasional morning in the local marketplace, where he would often meet Elijah the Prophet. One morning, when the market square was particularly crowded, Rabbi Beroka asked Elijah if anyone in the market was assured a place in heaven based on their actions.

Elijah pointed to a clean-shaven man of average height, dressed in the manner of the local peasantry. He was not wearing tzitzit, but he was wearing black shoes, which was most definitely not the Jewish fashion at the time. Surprised that such a man should be guaranteed a place in heaven, Rabbi Beroka went up to him and inquired, "What's your profession?"

"I work for the non-Jewish government as a jail keeper," the man replied. "I am careful to keep men and women separated for the protection of the women prisoners, and I am especially vigilant when it comes to the Jewish women in jail. I keep my Jewish identity secret so that I can influence the government on issues having to do with the Jewish community and warn the Jews of any impending decrees that would affect them."

Elijah then pointed out two more market goers who were destined for a place in heaven. They were taller than the first man and had a jolly presence about them. Rabbi Beroka approached them, too, and asked about their line of work.

"We are professional comedians," they answered. "We go to cheer up people who appear sad or depressed. Also, whenever we see two people who are angry at each other, we try hard to make peace between them."

ACTIVITY 2

Were you surprised by Elijah's selections? Explain your answer. _____

_____

_____

How did the jail keeper and the comedians turn their professions into social action?

_____

_____

TIKKUN OLAM SUPERSTAR: RABBANIT BRACHA KAPACH

They began as soft, incoherent moans, but the cries grew stronger every few minutes. When Rabbanit Bracha Kapach heard the faint sobs outside her Jerusalem apartment, she instinctively tossed aside the handkerchief she was embroidering and went quickly to investigate. *Will I find a victim of robbery or Arab violence?* she wondered nervously. For a split second, Bracha, a young Yemenite mother, whose two children were playing on the balcony, wished she had brought an embroidery needle for protection. That alien thought, contrary to her gentle nature, vanished like a desert mirage the moment she spied the old woman lying in the filth on the ground.

"Keep your hands off me," babbled the woman, as the rabbi's wife lifted her carefully. "Don't touch me!" she shrieked. Foul-smelling spittle sprayed from the woman's mouth onto Rabbanit Kapach's dress.

"It will be okay," comforted Rabbanit Kapach. "You're dehydrated and hungry; let me get you inside."

Rabbanit Bracha Kapach has dedicated her life to caring for the poor and downtrodden in Israel since this incident, which took place over sixty years ago. Her kindness knows no bounds—racial, economic, or ethnic. Through her untiring efforts, hundreds of people eat chicken each Shabbat; more than twenty thousand people receive food packages during Pesach; poor brides wear beautiful gowns at their weddings; and one hundred underprivileged children play at summer camp. Rabbanit Kapach's dedicated work on behalf of the needy is a moving example of *tikkun olam* in action and earned her the State of Israel's prestigious Israel Prize for her contributions to society.

> "How can a person sit at his Pesach table and not have helped someone else for the holiday?"

Learn the Lingo

Definition: *the activity of donating money, property, or volunteer work to needy people or institutions*

Give a specific example of philanthropy:

Use it in a sentence:

Philanthropy

How it applies to your life:

Definition: *the act of pleading for, supporting, or recommending a cause*

Give a specific example of advocacy:

Advocacy

Use it in a sentence:

How it applies to your life:

Complete the following charts with information about each *tikkun olam* vocabulary word. The definition has been completed for you.

Definition: *the practice of becoming actively involved in a cause, sometimes by demonstration or protest*

Give a specific example of activism:

Activism

Use it in a sentence:

How it applies to your life:

Definition: *service, usually as a volunteer, for the benefit of the public*

Give a specific example of community service:

Community service

Use it in a sentence:

How it applies to your life:

ACTIVITY 3

These four boxes are being donated to a local charity. What can you fill them with? Give three examples of items—tangible or not—that may belong inside.

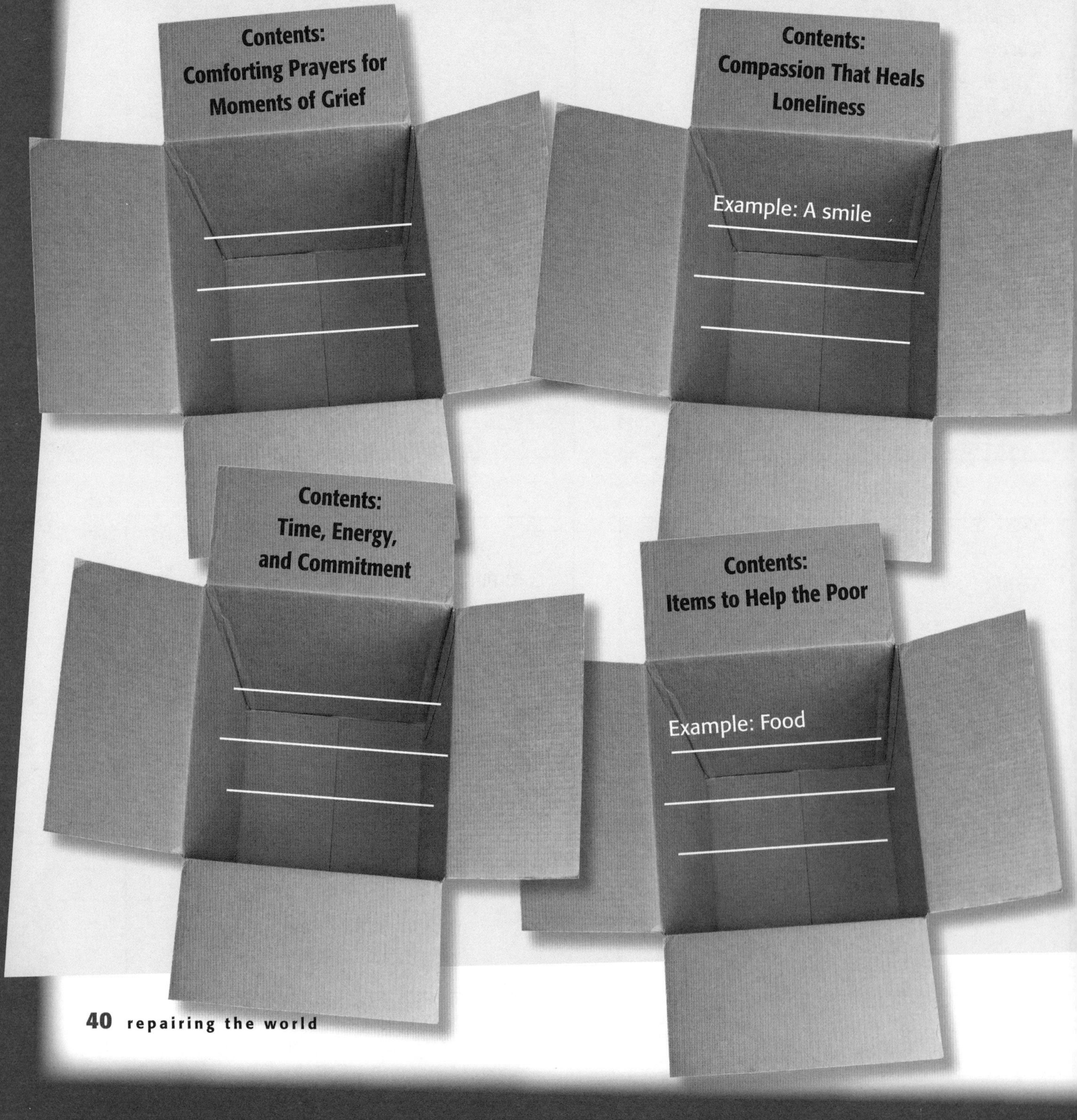

Contents:
Comforting Prayers for
Moments of Grief

_____

_____

_____

Contents:
Compassion That Heals
Loneliness

Example: A smile
_____

_____

_____

Contents:
Time, Energy,
and Commitment

_____

_____

_____

Contents:
Items to Help the Poor

Example: Food
_____

_____

_____

WHAT I THINK

"If you see what needs to be repaired and how to repair it, then you have found a piece of the world that God has left for you to complete."
(Rabbi Menachem Schneerson of Lubavitch)

1. Take a walk through your neighborhood. What is "broken" in your community?

2. What do you think is your personal responsibility for *tikkun olam*? How can you determine what broken bits of the world you would be best equipped to repair?

3. Why do you think that God has left parts of the world for people to repair? What does this show about our relationship with God?

4. Every repair person has a box of tools. What are the tools of *tikkun olam*? Create a tool kit—real or symbolic—to use in your *tikkun olam* work.

5. Start a "small change" tzedakah collection in the classroom. Where will you donate the money you collect? How will your coins help repair the world?

CONLUSION

In *Our Shared World,* which is the fourth volume in the *Living Jewish Values* series, we have explored these four Jewish values that connect us with our community:

Kehillah—Community
Tzedek—Justice
Arevut—Mutual Responsibility
Tikkun Olam—Repairing the World

In volume 3, *Be a Good Friend,* we introduced four values that build meaningful friendships:

Dan L'chaf Zechut—Judging Favorably
Reyut—Friendship
Koach Hadibur—The Power of Speech
Ometz Lev—Courage

In volume 2, *Family Connections,* we investigated four values that strengthen family relations:

Hakarat Hatov—Gratitude
Sh'lom Bayit—Family Harmony
Emet—Truth
Kedushah—Holiness

In volume 1, *Be Your Best Self,* we studied four values that foster personal growth:

K'vod Habriyot—Individual Dignity
T'shuvah—Returning to Your Best Self
Sameach B'chelko—Personal Satisfaction
Anavah—Humility

The dartboard below is divided into sixteen sections, one for each of the values we have discussed in the *Living Jewish Values series*. For each value, make an X in one area of the dartboard to represent how solidly you live by that value today. An X in the center of the board means that you are living fully by that particular Jewish value. An X far from center means that this is a value you need to review. Since there are sixteen values on the dartboard, you should make sixteen Xs.

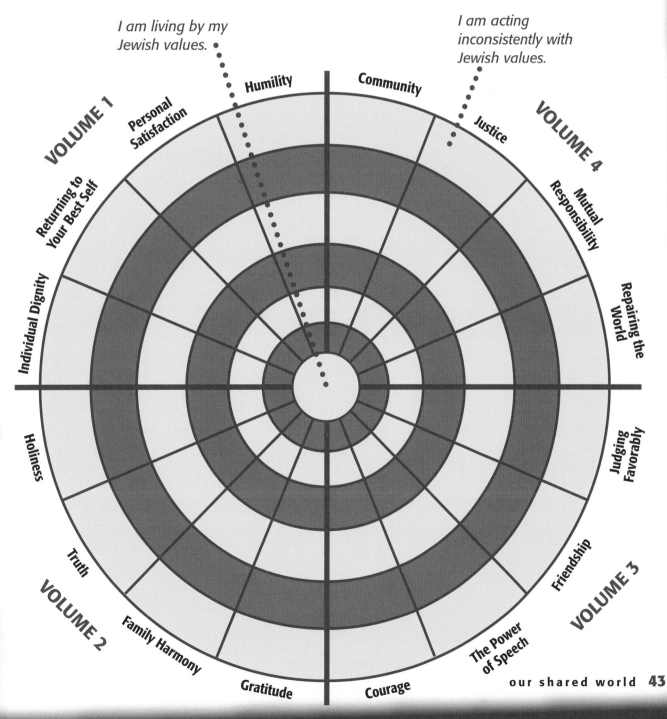

I am living by my Jewish values.

I am acting inconsistently with Jewish values.

Humility

Community

VOLUME 1

Personal Satisfaction

Justice

VOLUME 4

Returning to Your Best Self

Mutual Responsibility

Individual Dignity

Repairing the World

Holiness

Judging Favorably

Truth

Friendship

VOLUME 2

VOLUME 3

Family Harmony

The Power of Speech

Gratitude

Courage